DISGUSTING BUGS

BY PATRICK PERISH

EPIC

BELLWETHER MEDIA • MINNEAPOLIS, MN

EPIC BOOKS are no ordinary books. They burst with intense action, high-speed heroics, and shadows of the unknown. Are you ready for an Epic adventure?

This edition first published in 2015 by Bellwether Media, Inc.

No part of this publication may be reproduced in whole or in part without written permission of the publisher. For information regarding permission, write to Bellwether Media, Inc., Attention: Permissions Department, 5357 Penn Avenue South, Minneapolis, MN 55419.

Library of Congress Cataloging-in-Publication Data

Perish, Patrick, author.
 Disgusting Bugs / by Patrick Perish.
    pages cm. – (Epic. Totally Disgusting)
 Summary: "Engaging images accompany information about disgusting bugs. The combination of high-interest subject matter and light text is intended for students in grades 2 through 7"– Provided by publisher.
 Audience: Ages 7-12.
 Audience: Grades 2 to 7.
 Includes bibliographical references and index.
 ISBN 978-1-62617-128-2 (hardcover : alk. paper)
 ISBN 978-0-531-27221-3 (paperback : alk. paper)
 1. Insects–Juvenile literature. 2. Insects–Behavior–Juvenile literature. I. Title.
 QL467.2.P465 2014
 595.715–dc23

                         2014003686

Printed in the United States of America, North Mankato, MN.

TABLE OF CONTENTS

CREEPY CRAWLIES!

Forget about cute ladybugs and butterflies. Bugs are some of the grossest creatures on the planet. Some look out of this world. Others have gross **habits** and freaky abilities.

INSECT INVASION

There are more than one million different kinds of bugs. More are found every day.

GROSS BUG DEFENSES

Some bugs are gross as a **defense**. The stink bug looks harmless. But if it feels **threatened**, it releases a nasty **odor**. Some of them can even spray their stink.

GROSS-O-METER

Sort of
Disgusting

Totally
Disgusting

CONTROL FREAK

They can even
aim at their
attackers!

8

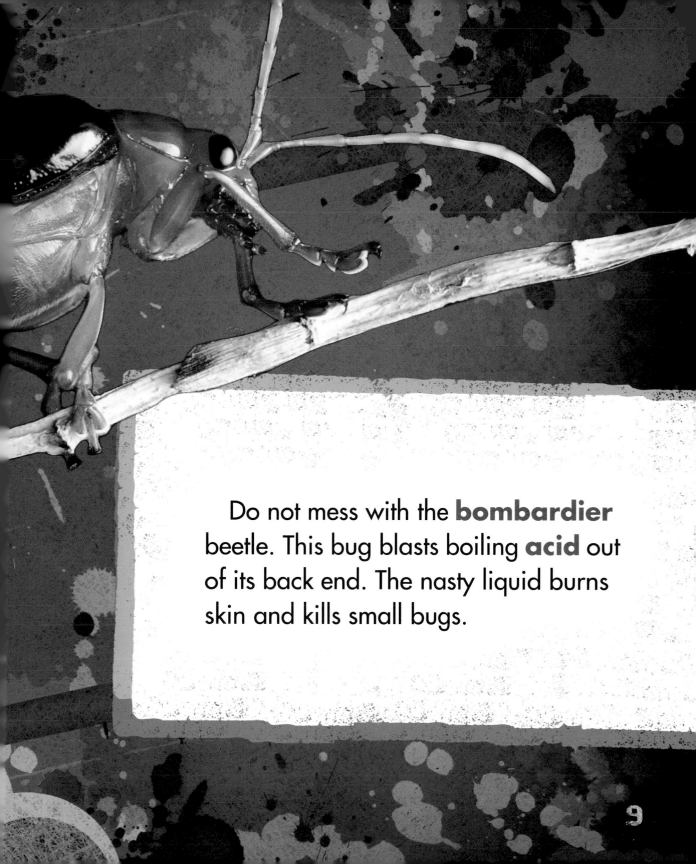

Do not mess with the **bombardier** beetle. This bug blasts boiling **acid** out of its back end. The nasty liquid burns skin and kills small bugs.

DISGUSTING INSTINCTS

Many bugs have gross **instincts**. Ticks are tiny blood suckers. These creepy crawlies are hard to see. They cling to people and animals and guzzle blood until they are full.

SICK SUCKERS

Some ticks can cause terrible sicknesses. They spread these through their bite.

Sort of Disgusting

Totally Disgusting

GROSS-O-METER

11

Sort of
Disgusting

Totally
Disgusting

GROSS-O-METER

MISSING SOMETHING?

A cockroach can live for a week without its head.

Cockroaches want to be your roommates. These speedy pests hide in dark places. They eat whatever they can find. Some hungry roaches even snack on books or hair!

Dung beetles come running when they smell fresh poop. They eat it, live in it, and lay their eggs in it.

Sort of Disgusting

Totally Disgusting

GROSS-O-METER

HOME SWEET HOME

Some beetles even roll dung into a big stinky ball. Then they roll their new treasure home.

MESSY EATERS

Some bugs are gross eaters.
Flies like to puke on their food.
The **vomit** turns the food into
mush. Then the flies slurp it up.

UGLY BABIES

Baby flies look like squirmy white worms. They eat fruits, meat, and even dung.

GROSS-O-METER

Sort of Disgusting

Totally Disgusting

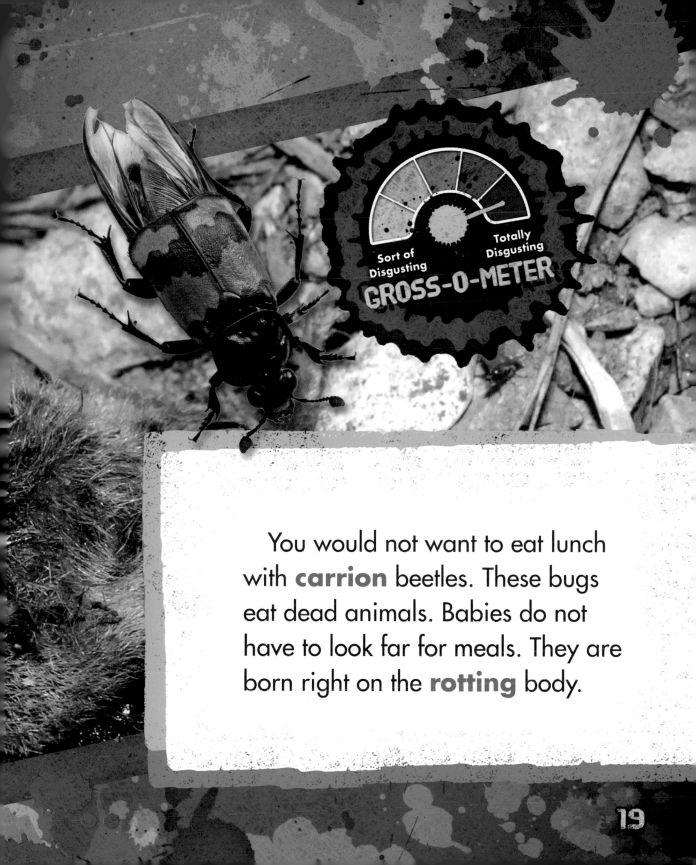

Sort of
Disgusting

Totally
Disgusting

GROSS-O-METER

You would not want to eat lunch
with **carrion** beetles. These bugs
eat dead animals. Babies do not
have to look far for meals. They are
born right on the **rotting** body.

The centipede looks like something out of a nightmare. Its many legs help it scuttle after small bugs. Then it attacks with **venom** claws. Yikes!

Sort of Disgusting

Totally Disgusting

GROSS-O-METER

MONSTER MOUTH

Giant centipedes grow more than 1 foot (30 centimeters) long. These giants eat birds and mice.

21

GLOSSARY

acid—a sour liquid; some acids can be dangerous.

bombardier—a person who launches bombs; bombardier beetles spray acid from their back ends.

carrion—the rotting meat of dead animals

defense—protection from harm

dung—animal poop

habits—repeated behaviors

instincts—the skills and knowledge that an animal is born with

odor—a smell; some bugs use odors as a defense.

rotting—decomposing or falling apart

threatened—afraid of being hurt

venom—a poison created by a centipede; centipedes deliver venom through their front claws.

vomit—a mixture of stomach acids, mucus, and food

TO LEARN MORE

At the Library

Honovich, Nancy, and Darlyne Murawski. *Ultimate Bug-opedia: The Most Complete Bug Reference Ever.* Washington, D.C.: National Geographic Kids, 2013.

Kravetz, Jonathan. *Cockroaches.* New York, N.Y.: PowerKids Press, 2006.

Miller, Connie Colwell. *Disgusting Bugs.* Mankato, Minn.: Capstone Press, 2007.

On the Web

Learning more about disgusting bugs is as easy as 1, 2, 3.

1. Go to www.factsurfer.com.

2. Enter "disgusting bugs" into the search box.

3. Click the "Surf" button and you will see a list of related web sites.

With factsurfer.com, finding more information is just a click away.

INDEX

The images in this book are reproduced through the courtesy of: Scruggelgreen, front cover (top left); seeyou, front cover (top right); Four Oaks, front cover (bottom), Scholastic cover; Kesu, pp. 4-5; gosphotodesign, pp. 4 (bottom), 12 (middle); paulrommer, p. 5 (top); Sarah2, p. 5 (middle); Reinhold Leitner, p. 5 (middle right); Eric Isselee, p. 5 (bottom right); Arto Hakola, pp. 6-7; johannviloria, pp. 8-9; Kalcutta, p. 10 (small); Risto0, pp. 10-11; Jiri Hera, p. 12 (bottom left); smuay, p. 12 (top left); D. Kucharski K. Kucharska, p. 13 (top); Chichinkin, pp. 12-13; Neal Cooper, pp. 14-15; PhilipYb, pp. 16-17; Sergey Goruppa, p. 17 (bottom); Jason P. Ross, pp. 18-19; Tobyphotos, p. 9; Boonroong, p. 20; kamnuan, pp. 20-21; Tsekhmister, p. 21 (bottom).